ROSEN Verified

THE BILL OF RIGHTS

What Is the Right to Bear Arms?

Kathleen A. Klatte

ROSEN PUBLISHING

Published in 2024 by The Rosen Publishing Group, Inc.
2544 Clinton Street, Buffalo, NY 14224

First Edition

Editor: Greg Roza
Book Design: Michael Flynn

Photo Credits: Cover Nomad_Soul/Shutterstock.com; (series background) PinkPueblo/Shutterstock.com; p. 5 Jacob Lund/Shutterstock.com; pp. 7, 13 Everett Collection/Shutterstock.com; p. 9 https://commons.wikimedia.org/wiki/File:Interview_of_Samoset_with_the_Pilgrims.jpg; p. 11 jejim/Shutterstock.com; p. 15 (bottom) Jim Lambert/Shutterstock.com; p. 15 (top) https://commons.wikimedia.org/wiki/File:British_Military_Short_Land_Pattern_Musket.jpg; p. 17 Julian Stratenschulte/picture-alliance/dpa/AP Images; p. 19 sirtravelalot/Shutterstock.com; p. 20 Martynova Anna/Shutterstock.com; p. 21 Vera Larina/Shutterstock.com; p. 23 Robert Nyholm/Shutterstock.com; p. 24 PHOTOOBJECT/Shutterstock.com; p. 25 Harry Collins Photography/Shutterstock.com; p. 27 Frame Stock Footage/Shutterstock.com; p. 29 (top) Tinnaporn Sathapornnanont/Shutterstock.com; p. 29 (bottom) https://commons.wikimedia.org/wiki/File:Supreme_Court_of_the_United_States_-_Roberts_Court_2022.jpg; p. 31 https://commons.wikimedia.org/wiki/File:Antonin_Scalia_Official_SCOTUS_Portrait.jpg; p. 33 Keith Homan/Shutterstock.com; p. 35 Wirestock Creators/Shutterstock.com; p. 36 Miguel G. Saavedra/Shutterstock.com; p. 37 Nic Neufeld/Shutterstock.com; p. 39 Michael Bordon/Shutterstock.com; p. 40 DanielJohn/Shutterstock.com; p. 43 https://en.wikipedia.org/wiki/File:P20220707AS-1381_(52308218001).jpg; p. 45 Darrenp/Shutterstock.com.

Cataloging-in-Publication Data

Names: Klatte, Kathleen A.
Title: What is the right to bear arms? / Kathleen A. Klatte.
Description: New York : Rosen Publishing, 2024. | Series: Rosen verified: the Bill of Rights | Includes glossary and index.
Identifiers: ISBN 9781499469660 (pbk.) | ISBN 9781499469677 (library bound) | ISBN 9781499469684 (ebook)
Subjects: LCSH: United States. Constitution. 2nd Amendment--Juvenile literature. | Firearms--Law and legislation--United States--History--Juvenile literature. | Gun control--United States--History--Juvenile literature. | Firearms--Licenses--United States--Juvenile literature.
Classification: LCC KF3941.K53 2024 | DDC 344.7305'33--dc23

Manufactured in the United States of America

Some of the images in this book illustrate individuals who are models. The depictions do not imply actual situations or events.

CPSIA Compliance Information: Batch #CSRYA24. For further information contact Rosen Publishing at 1-800-237-9932.

CONTENTS

The Second Amendment

"A well-regulated **militia**, being necessary to the security of a free state, the right of the people to keep and bear arms, shall not be **infringed**."

One sentence. Twenty-six words. Those few words have caused some big arguments. Like many early laws, the Second Amendment was written in **reaction** to things done by the British government to the American colonies.

The Founding Fathers lived in a very different world than we do. People in the 18th century often needed guns to defend their homes, or keep them safe. There were no police as we know them now and no way to quickly call for help.

Many people were afraid that a standing army could be used against them. They thought having local militias was a better idea.

Today we have police departments and telephones with which to call them. We have armed forces to **protect** our country. So why do people argue about having guns?

Many people feel it's too easy to get a powerful gun. They want stronger gun control laws.

The Bill of Rights

Article V of the United States **Constitution** allows for amendments, or changes, to be made. The first 10 amendments to the Constitution are called the Bill of Rights. These are rights that the founders considered so important that they needed to be spelled out. In fact, several founders refused to sign the Constitution until a Bill of Rights was added.

The Bill of Rights guarantees, or promises, freedom of speech and other things. It also protects the rights of people accused of, or blamed for, crimes.

The Bill of Rights was written by James Madison. The final amendments were ratified, or approved, in 1791. He was inspired, or given ideas, by the Virginia Declaration of Rights. That was written by George Mason and adopted in 1776.

BILL OF RIGHTS

1. Freedom of speech, press, and religion
2. Right to bear arms
3. No quartering (housing) of soldiers
4. Freedom from unreasonable searches and seizures (taking of property)
5. Right to due process of law
6. Rights of accused persons
7. Right of trial by jury in civil cases
8. Freedom from cruel and unusual punishments
9. Other rights of the people
10. Powers reserved to the states

James Madison

Colonial America

Colonial America was a very different society from what we're used to. Many people lived on farms, often miles from the nearest town. Farmers had to protect their livestock from predators, or wild animals. People also needed guns to hunt for food.

Sometimes, governments in Europe argued about which colonies belonged to them. The people living in these colonies might have had to deal with enemy soldiers.

All of these were very good reasons for colonial people to have guns to protect their homes and families.

COLONISTS COULDN'T CALL 9-1-1!

The first modern police force wasn't formed until 1844. Some large colonial cities had night watchmen. They were often paid by private citizens and not the city. There were no phones with which to call for help. There were no police cars to go to crime scenes.

European colonists often settled on lands where Native Americans had lived for hundreds of years. The two groups often had very different ideas about this. Sometimes these disagreements became **violent**.

Revolutionary America

People in colonial America didn't like the idea of standing professional, or paid, armies. Some kings in Europe at the time would use their armies to force people to do what they wanted. The founders thought that the military should answer to a government elected by citizens. They thought it was better for people to be able to defend themselves. If needed, they could come together to form a militia for protection.

RIGHTS AND RULES

- The English Bill of Rights (1689) said that citizens had the right to protect themselves. It was limited to members of the Protestant religion.
- The Declaration of Independence (1776) argues against the English king maintaining, or keeping, standing armies in the colonies.
- The Third Amendment (1791) prohibits, or bans, the government from housing soldiers in people's homes in peacetime.

The minutemen were members of local colonial militias. They were required by law to own a gun and defend their town. They trained to be ready to fight at a minute's notice.

Life in a New Nation

At the end of the Revolutionary War, people in the new United States had different ideas about what form their new government should take. Some people thought they needed a strong federal, or central, government to protect the new nation from outside threats, or dangers. These people were called Federalists.

Other people were afraid of strong central governments. They didn't want to maintain a professional army. They were used to European kings using powerful armies to do whatever the kings wanted. These people thought it was important to protect the rights of each state. They were called Anti-Federalists.

By the time of the Revolutionary War, the northern and southern colonies had very different ways of life. The southern **economy** was based on large farms called plantations that used enslaved people for labor. The northern economy was based more on factories and businesses.

EQUALITY FOR ALL?

Today, most people think "We the People," the opening words of the U.S. Constitution, means everyone. In 1791, the founders really only thought about protecting the rights of white men. Sometimes this meant only white men who owned property. Equal protection under the law wasn't promised to all citizens until the 14th Amendment was adopted in 1868.

FOURTEENTH AMENDMENT

This amendment states that "No State shall . . . deny to any person within its **jurisdiction** the equal protection of the laws."

Guns in the 18th Century

The guns people used when the Second Amendment was written were very different from the ones people can get today. Guns could only fire one bullet at a time. The gun had to be reloaded to fire another shot. Reloading the gun meant putting in another bullet by hand. Some kinds of guns needed a bullet and gunpowder for each shot. People had to practice to be able to reload quickly. They might have been able to fire two or three shots in a minute.

KINDS OF GUNS

Rifles and pistols are two common types of guns. Pistols are handguns with a short barrel. Rifles are long guns that are held to the shoulder. There are also revolvers, shotguns, and more kinds.

BROWN BESS

One of the most commonly used weapons during the Revolutionary War was the "Brown Bess." This was a British-designed, muzzle-loading gun. "Muzzle-loading" means the musket ball had to be loaded into the firing end of the gun, or muzzle, and pushed into place with a rod. Most of these guns could have a blade called a bayonet on the firing end.

Eighteenth-century people didn't just go to a store and buy boxes of bullets. Musket balls were made at home. Lead was melted down in a fire and molded into balls.

America Today

Today, more people live in large cities and towns. People who live in **rural** areas also have phones and cars.

There are thousands of professional police officers in the United States. There are local, county, state, and federal police forces. People can call for help on their cell phones wherever and whenever they're in trouble. Police can go to emergencies, or cases when people need sudden help, in cars, motorcycles, and even boats or helicopters. Federal police protect our borders. Military forces protect us from other armies.

TERRORIST ATTACKS

Some people argue that they need guns to defend themselves from **terrorists**. The worst terrorist attacks on U.S. soil were the September 11, 2001, al-Qaeda attacks. The terrorists crashed planes into buildings. Do you think private citizens with guns could have stopped that from happening?

Today, when many Americans need help, they dial 9-1-1. Computers help the 9-1-1 operator contact the police or fire department. The system is always being upgraded with new **technology**.

Personal Rights vs. Public Safety

Many people think that the Constitution guarantees them the right to own, carry, and use guns. They say they feel safer if they're armed. They want to defend their own homes. They point out that at the time the Constitution was written, most men were required to own a gun to defend their town when needed.

Other people think that there should be many careful laws about who can buy guns and where they can carry them. They argue that we have police and the military to defend us. They believe there would be fewer mass shootings if guns were harder to buy.

VERIFIED

The American Civil Liberties Union (ACLU) is an organization that exists to protect people's constitutional rights. It says that the right to bear arms should have reasonable limits. It also says gun control laws should be fair and equal. To learn more, visit the ACLU website: **www.aclu.org**.

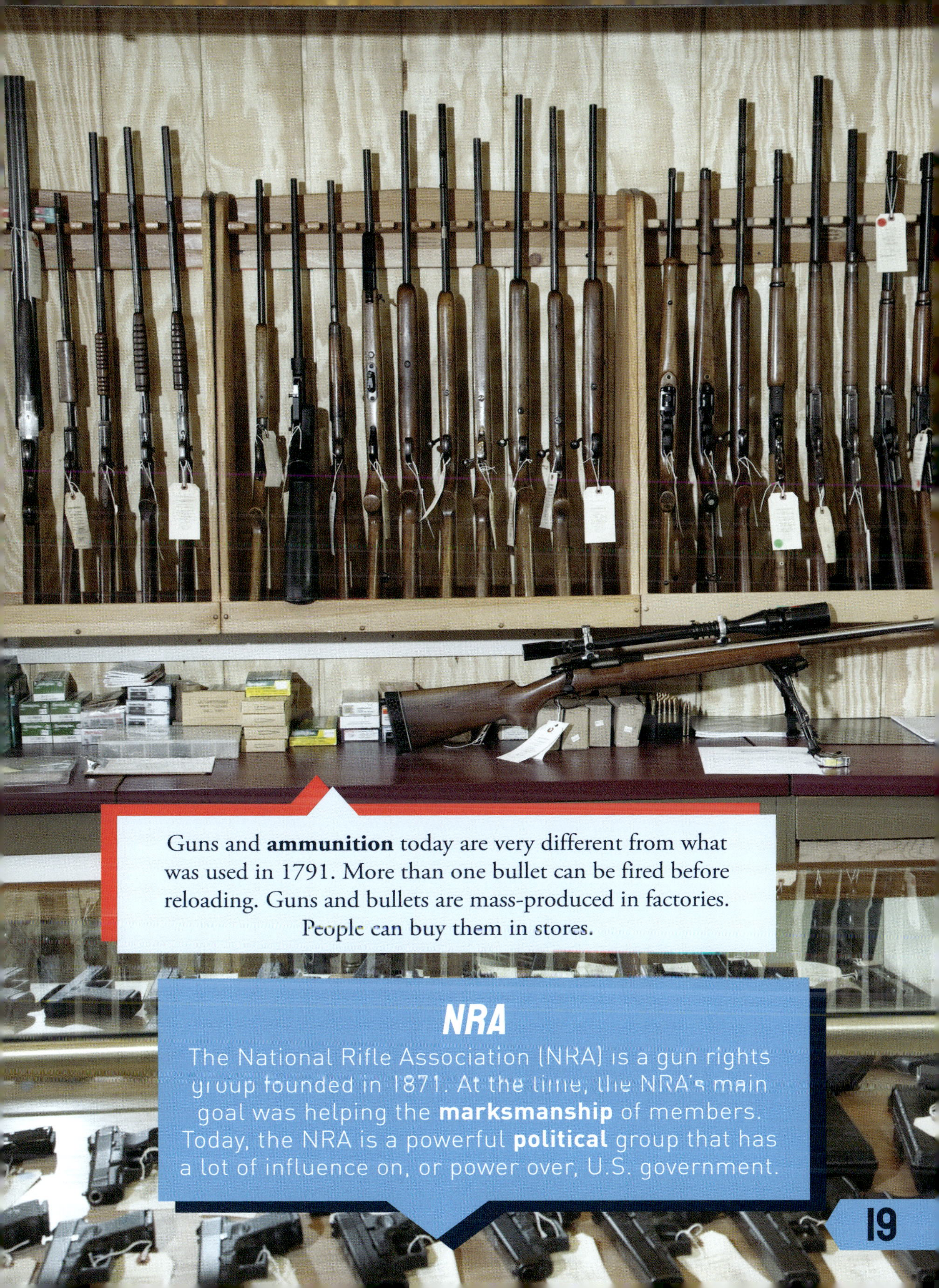

Guns and **ammunition** today are very different from what was used in 1791. More than one bullet can be fired before reloading. Guns and bullets are mass-produced in factories. People can buy them in stores.

NRA

The National Rifle Association (NRA) is a gun rights group founded in 1871. At the time, the NRA's main goal was helping the **marksmanship** of members. Today, the NRA is a powerful **political** group that has a lot of influence on, or power over, U.S. government.

Guns for Sport

Shooting has been a popular sport for centuries. Today, there are events at all levels from local to international. Shooting contests involve shooting at fixed **targets** with rifles and pistols. They also include shooting at flying clay targets with shotguns. Shooting events have been part of the Olympics since the first modern games in 1896.

Biathlon is a winter sport that combines cross-country skiing and target shooting. It began as a style of military action in Scandinavian countries. It was used in combat, or fighting, in the 18th century. Now it's an Olympic sport.

VERIFIED
USA Shooting is the governing body for sports shooting events in the United States. You can find out more at **usashooting.org**.

Clay target shooting is also known as clay pigeon shooting. Long ago, this sport used live pigeons instead of clay targets.

The Boy Scouts have sport shooting programs for kids. The programs are meant to teach responsible, or safe, gun handling as well as marksmanship. The NRA holds thousands of contests for shooters of all levels.

Hunting

Before the first European colonists arrived, North America had far more wilderness, or wild, areas. Many kinds of animals lived on the land. Many Native peoples tried to work with nature. They didn't use more than they needed.

Colonists cleared large areas for farming and building. They killed animals for fur or meat or because they killed livestock.

Today, most wilderness areas in the United States are fairly small. They often don't have a healthy balance of predators and prey, or the animals they eat. Modern hunters help to keep the numbers of prey animals small enough to live well in the space they have left.

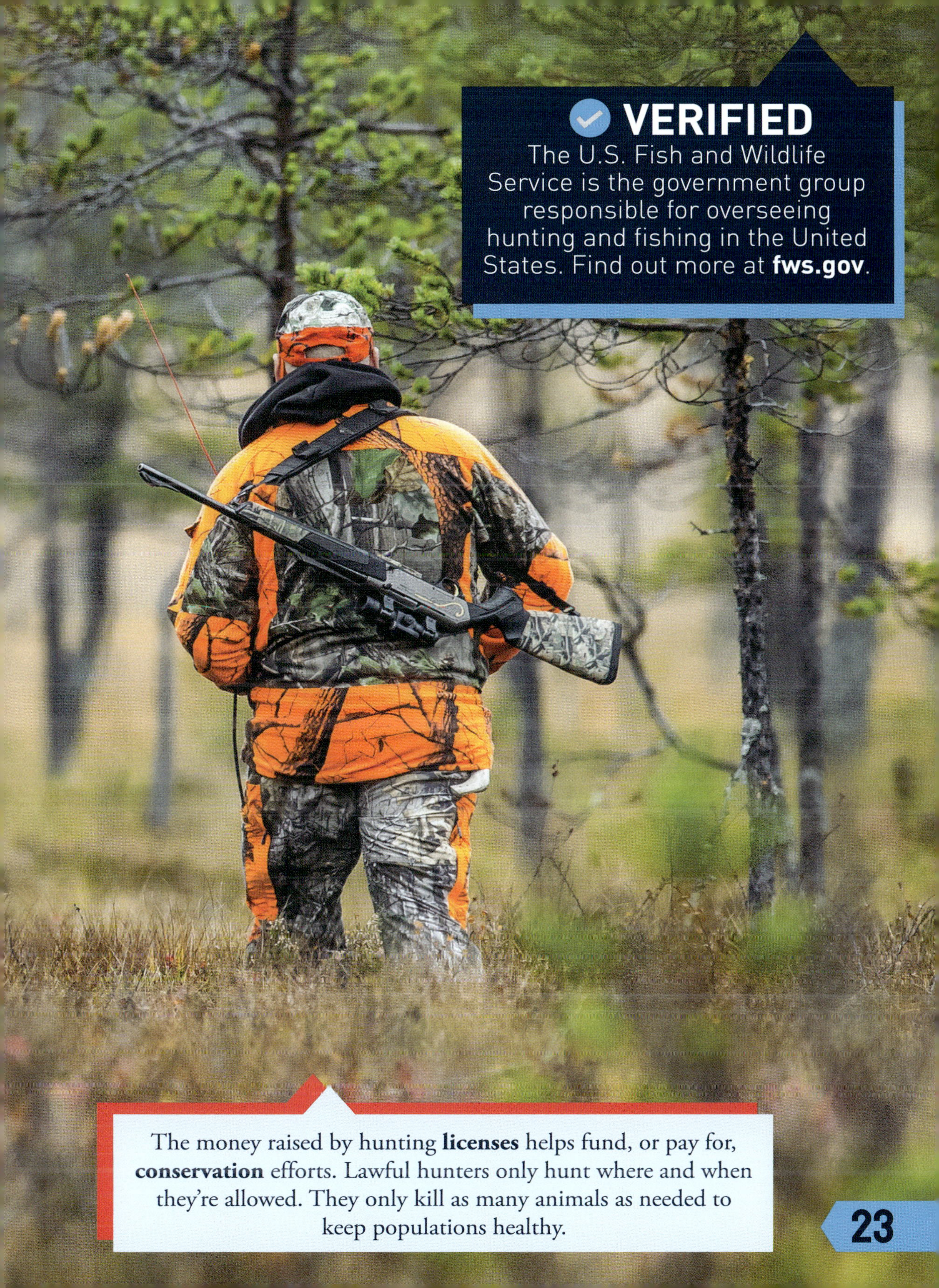

VERIFIED

The U.S. Fish and Wildlife Service is the government group responsible for overseeing hunting and fishing in the United States. Find out more at **fws.gov**.

The money raised by hunting **licenses** helps fund, or pay for, **conservation** efforts. Lawful hunters only hunt where and when they're allowed. They only kill as many animals as needed to keep populations healthy.

Protecting Livestock

Farming today is different in many ways from what the founders knew. However, some things remain the same. Where there are livestock, there will be predators that want to eat them. Coyotes, wolves, foxes, mountain lions, and bears are known to kill farm animals. This costs the farmers money.

Some of the animals that prey on livestock are protected by law. For example, shooting bald eagles isn't just bad for the **environment**—it's illegal.

Farmers have used guns to kill predators for centuries. However, predators are an important part of nature. Removing too many hurts the environment. Scientists today suggest chasing away predators with electric fences, bright lights, and loud sounds rather than using guns.

A Well-Regulated Militia

The Second Amendment talks about a "well-regulated militia." There are many arguments about exactly what that means today.

The National Guard is similar in some ways to the colonial militia units. Guard members live and work in their communities instead of at military bases. The governor of their state calls them to action as needed. Guard units train one weekend a month, plus two weeks a year. They can be deployed, or sent, to different kinds of emergencies.

Reservists are also military personnel who serve part-time. However, they aren't sent to civilian, or noncombat, emergencies.

Today's military uses the latest technology. This technology can track troop movements from space.

Who Decides?

The U.S. Supreme Court is the most important court in the country. It doesn't hear the sort of cases you see on TV shows. It decides if laws are constitutional. Part of its job is to make sure that laws still work as society changes. For example, in 1896, the Supreme Court ruled that **segregation** was legal. That decision was reversed, or changed, in 1954.

The Supreme Court often makes decisions about the limits of Americans' rights. The First Amendment guarantees free speech, but there are consequences, or results, for saying untrue things that cause harm to other people.

FAMOUS CASE

U.S. v. Miller was an important case the Supreme Court ruled on in 1939. It said that weapons like sawed-off shotguns weren't protected by the Second Amendment. This is because they're not weapons used by a well-regulated militia.

VERIFIED

You can learn more about the United States Supreme Court at **supremecourt.gov**.

The current Supreme Court justices are a mix of men and women. They were selected by presidents from both major political parties.

Federal vs. Local

The United States is a very large country. Weather and environment can be very different from state to state. People often live very different lives. What seems good in one state might not seem to make sense in another. It can be hard to agree on laws.

The Supreme Court makes decisions that affect the laws for all Americans. If a state makes a law that goes against the Constitution or other federal law, the Supreme Court can overturn it. This part of the Constitution is called the supremacy clause.

KEY CASES

These are cases where local law took away a right guaranteed by the Constitution. The Supreme Court overturned the local laws.

2008 - *Heller v. District of Columbia*

A person has the right to keep handguns in their own home. (Overturned D.C.'s handgun ban.)

2010 - *McDonald v. City of Chicago*

Overturned Chicago's complete handgun ban.

Justice Antonin Scalia (1936–2016) wrote that "Like most rights, the right secured by the Second Amendment is not unlimited. [It is] not a right to keep and carry any weapon whatsoever in any manner whatsoever and for whatever purpose."

The Influence of the NRA

One of the National Rifle Association's major goals is to protect the rights of lawful gun owners. The NRA teaches people about guns and how to use them safely. It offers training for hunters, contest shooters, and police officers. Its Eddie Eagle GunSafe program teaches young children what to do if they find a gun.

Today the NRA is known as a major voice for the rights of Americans to own firearms. Its leaders say the Second Amendment guarantees people the right to defend themselves. They talk to politicians about laws that affect guns.

LOBBYISTS

The NRA is a political lobby. A lobby is a group that tries to influence lawmakers. Lobbyists give money to politicians who agree with their ideas. They work against laws they think are wrong.

VERIFIED
Find out more about the NRA at **www.nra.org**.

Many people feel that the NRA is too powerful. They think it has too much influence on laws and politics. Some people choose to work against the NRA.

Buying a Gun

Laws about buying guns are different from state to state and sometimes from one area of a state to another. Some places require the completion of a safety class before someone can buy a gun. Others require an interview, or talk, with law enforcement members.

Generally, a person purchasing a gun needs to provide government-issued identification, or something that proves who they are. They must go through a background check. The legal age to buy a gun might be 18 or 21, depending on the type of gun. In some places, there's a waiting period to complete the purchase.

WAIT!

Some people think a waiting period before buying a gun is a good idea. It gives law enforcement time to complete a background check. It also may help stop people from buying guns when they're angry or upset. However, others argue that this doesn't stop people who are planning to do something dangerous.

VERIFIED

The Bureau of Alcohol, Tobacco, Firearms, and Explosives (ATF) is a federal law enforcement agency. It tracks legal gun sales in the United States. You can learn more about it at **atf.gov**.

Gun shows are large public events. They may include private sellers as well as licensed gun dealers. Sales can sometimes occur without proper background checks or waiting periods.

Responsible Gun Ownership

At the time the Constitution was written, guns served many useful purposes in daily American life. They were found in most homes, and children were taught to handle them from a young age.

Today, guns are much more powerful. They're no longer used as a daily tool. The safest way to store a gun is unloaded and in a locked case or safe. Ammunition should be stored in a separate locked case. In some places, laws require guns to be stored this way, especially in homes where children live.

This gun is fitted with a safety lock. The lock requires a key to open. It can't be fired accidentally, or without meaning to.

Licenses and Permits

Licenses or permits are required to make, sell, carry, or use guns. There are many different types. They're issued at different levels of government.

The ATF issues federal permits for dealers, manufacturers, and **importers** of firearms and ammunition.

Licenses or permits for people to have or carry guns are issued by local government. These include people such as police or security guards who use guns for work. This also includes hunters. Restrictions, or rules, tend to be tougher for handguns, because they can be hidden easily.

DOES EVERYONE NEED A PERMIT?

Some states have "constitutional carry" or permitless concealed carry laws. This means that a person doesn't need a special license to carry a concealed weapon in public. They still need to be of legal age to own a gun.

A concealed carry permit allows a person to carry a concealed, or hidden, gun in public. The gun is most often carried in a holster, or case, or bag. The gun should always be secured so it can't fire accidentally.

Mass shootings are scary in part because they can happen anywhere. There have been shootings in supermarkets, schools, and dance clubs. Those shot have included old people, kids, and teachers. People all over the country see them on the news. It makes some people afraid to go out or send their kids to school.

Mass Shootings

A mass shooting is generally considered to be an event in which at least four people are shot. The Rockefeller Institute of Government further calls it an event not connected with gang or terrorist activity.

Some shootings seem to be motivated, or caused, by **racism** or other forms of **prejudice**. Many seem to come from feelings of anger, whether toward a certain group or in general.

The United States has more mass shootings than any other country. It's also one of the few countries in the world that considers gun ownership a basic right.

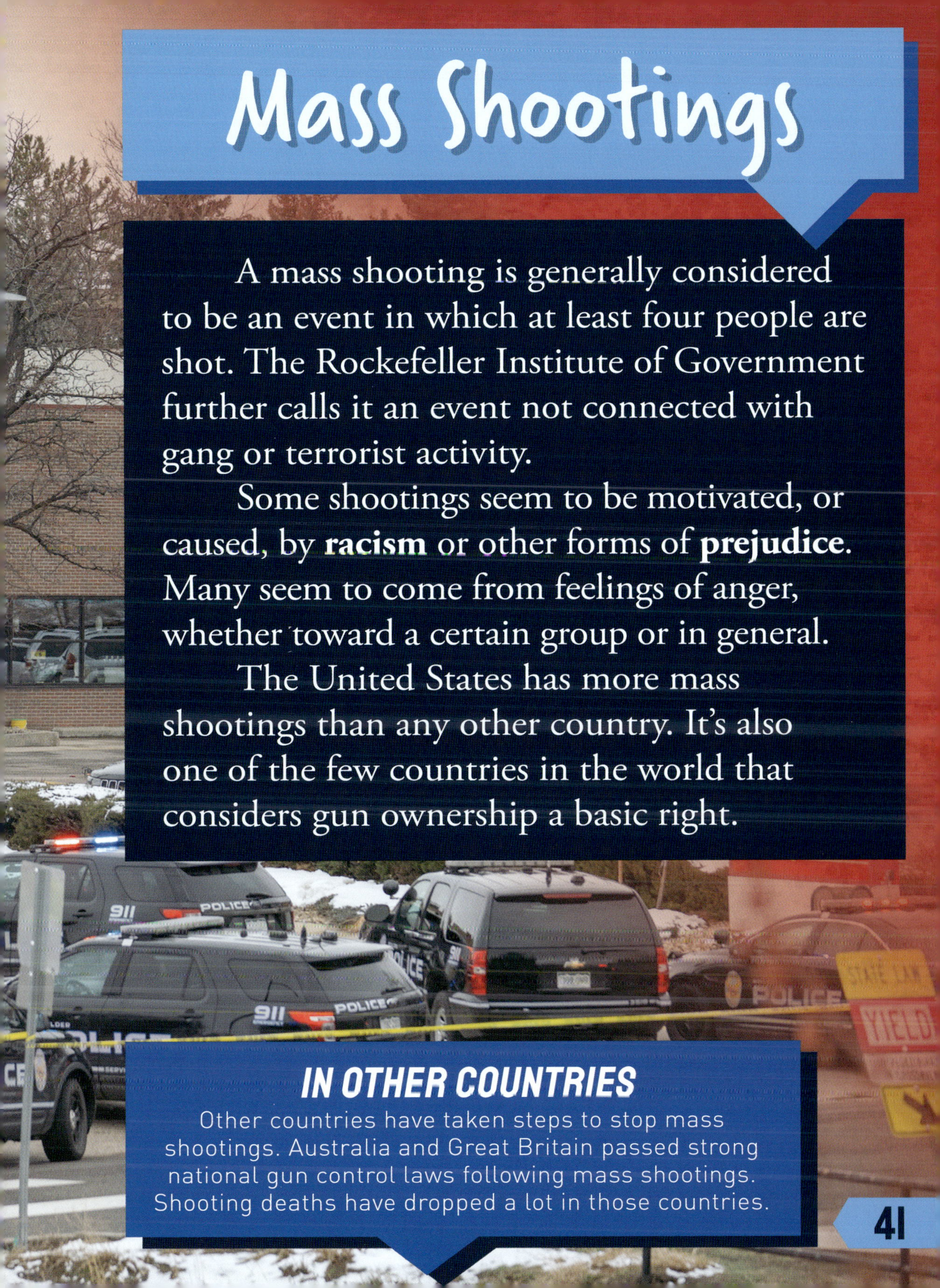

IN OTHER COUNTRIES

Other countries have taken steps to stop mass shootings. Australia and Great Britain passed strong national gun control laws following mass shootings. Shooting deaths have dropped a lot in those countries.

Gun Control Lobby Groups

There are many groups in the United States that try to influence lawmakers to pass tougher gun control laws. They raise money, make public service announcements (PSAs), and hold public meetings.

Sandy Hook Promise was founded by families of those killed in a deadly shooting at Sandy Hook Elementary School. The shooter killed 26 people. Twenty of them were young children.

VERIFIED

You can learn more about Sandy Hook Promise at its website: **www.sandyhookpromise.org**.

VERIFIED

March for Our Lives is a group formed by young people. They want to change gun laws. The group was founded in reaction to a school shooting in Florida. You can find out more at **marchforourlives.com**.

PASSING LAWS

The Bipartisan Safer Communities Act was signed into law by President Biden on June 25, 2022. It provides money for school safety programs in communities. It also makes it harder for criminals to buy guns.

Gabby Giffords

President Joe Biden

Giffords Law Center was cofounded by former congresswoman Gabby Giffords. She was the victim of gun violence herself. A gunman opened fire at an event where she was speaking. He killed six people and wounded 12 others.

An Ongoing Debate

When the Founding Fathers formed the U.S. government, they considered what they didn't like about being colonists and tried to correct those things. They studied citizens' rights. Most importantly, they created the Constitution so that it could be changed as needed. Some things that made perfect sense in the 18th century just don't work anymore.

Most people no longer use firearms as tools for daily life. Guns available today are much more deadly than the ones the founders knew. On the other side, some people say the Second Amendment still protects the right to protect oneself however a person wants.

In 1791, there were arguments about states' rights versus the federal government. Today the question seems to be: which do we value more—personal rights, or the safety of society in general? This is a question that will continue to be important in the coming years.

After a mass shooting in New Zealand, the government passed tough gun control laws. People decided that society's right to be safe is more important than a person's right to own any kind of gun they want.

GLOSSARY

ammunition: The objects (such as bullets and shells) that are shot from weapons.

conservation: Efforts to care for the natural world.

constitution: The basic laws by which a country, state, or group is governed.

economy: The process or system by which goods and services are produced, sold, and bought in a country or region.

environment: The natural world around us.

import: To bring in from another country.

infringe: To wrongly limit or restrict something, such as another person's rights.

jurisdiction: The limits or territory within which a person or group can exercise authority.

license: An official paper giving someone the right to do something.

marksmanship: Skill in shooting guns.

militia: A group of people who are not part of the armed forces of a country but are trained like soldiers.

political: Having to do with politics, or the activities of the government and government officials.

prejudice: An unfair feeling of dislike for a person or group because of race, sex, religion, etc.

protect: To keep safe.

racism: The belief that one group or race of people is better than another group or race.

reaction: A response to something that happens, such as a change.

rural: Of or relating to the country and the people who live there.

segregation: The separation of people based on race, class, sex, gender, or ethnicity.

target: Something to be aimed at.

technology: A method that uses science to solve problems and the tools used to solve those problems.

terrorist: A person who uses violence to scare people as a way of achieving a political goal.

violent: Involving using physical force to harm or damage.

INDEX